AXIS PARENT GUIDES SERIES

PARENT GUIDE BUNDLES

A PARENT'S GUIDE TO DEPRESSION & ANXIETY

A PARENT'S GUIDE TO

DEPRESSION & ANXIETY

axis

Tyndale House Publishers
Carol Stream, Illinois

Visit Tyndale online at tyndale.com.

A Parent's Guide to Depression & Anxiety

Designed by Lindsey Bergsma

For information about special discounts for bulk purchases, please contact Tyndale House Publishers at csresponse@tyndale.com, or call 1-855-277-9400.

Library of Congress Cataloging-in-Publication Data

A catalog record for this book is available from the Library of Congress.

ISBN 978-1-4964-6770-6

Printed in the United States of America

29	28	27	26	25	24	23
7	6	5	4	3	2	1

Every child, every person needs to know that they are a source of joy; every child, every person, needs to be celebrated. Only when all of our weaknesses are accepted as part of our humanity can our negative, broken self-images be transformed.

JEAN VANIER, *BECOMING HUMAN*

CONTENTS

A LETTER FROM AXIS

Dear Reader,

We're Axis, and since 2007, we've been creating resources to help connect parents, teens, and Jesus in a disconnected world. We're a group of gospel-minded researchers, speakers, and content creators, and we're excited to bring you the best of what we've learned about making meaningful connections with the teens in your life.

This parent's guide is designed to help start a conversation. Our goal is to give you enough knowledge that you're able to ask your teen informed questions about their world. For each guide, we spend weeks reading, researching, and interviewing parents and teens in order to distill everything you need to know about the topic at hand. We encourage you to read the whole thing and then to use the questions we include to get the conversation going with your teen—and then to follow the conversation wherever it leads.

As Douglas Stone, Bruce Patton, and Sheila Heen point out in their book *Difficult Conversations*, "Changes in attitudes and behavior rarely come about because of arguments, facts, and attempts to persuade. How often do *you* change your values and beliefs—or whom you love or what you want in life—based on something someone tells you? And how likely are you to do so when the person who is trying to change you doesn't seem fully aware of the reasons you see things differently in the first place?"[1] For whatever reason, when we believe that others are trying to understand *our* point of view, our defenses usually go down, and we're more willing to listen to *their* point of view. The rising generation is no exception.

So we encourage you to ask questions, to listen, and then to share your heart with your teen. As we often say at Axis, discipleship happens where conversation happens.

Sincerely,
Your friends at Axis

---

[1] Douglas Stone, Bruce Patton, and Sheila Heen, *Difficult Conversations: How to Discuss What Matters Most*, rev. ed. (New York: Penguin Books, 2010), 137.

THE "BLACK DOG"

TEENS TEST-DRIVE a variety of emotions every day, and sometimes they have no idea how to explain or express them. We've all heard (or even said) something like, "I'm so depressed! They canceled my favorite show!" or "I'm so anxious about my math test!" The language of mental illness runs rampant through our casual conversations. It's not all that surprising, though. These days it's like everyone on earth has a microphone, and with the racket of everyone's opinions, hyperbole seems a useful method for getting heard. The louder the noise, the less others want to listen, so we sometimes use exaggerations to describe how we feel and to connect with others.

But things like depression and anxiety are no exaggerations. Rick Warren, pastor of one of the largest evangelical churches in the US and author of one of the top bestsellers in history (*The Purpose Driven Life*), lost his son Matthew to suicide after a long battle with a serious depression disorder. Author, pastor, and Southern Baptist Convention president Frank Page wrote a well-read book about his daughter's severe depression and eventual suicide. A quarter of pastors (yes, *pastors*) admit to having suffered from mental illness themselves—most often depression or anxiety, and many of them since childhood.[1] Even Winston Churchill suffered terribly from a lifelong untreated mood disorder he called a "black dog" that would sit on his lap and haunt him.[2]

Let's talk about this "black dog" and how you can help your teen more effectively cope and find healing.

A quarter of pastors (yes, *pastors*) admit to having suffered from mental illness themselves— most often depression or anxiety, and many of them since childhood.

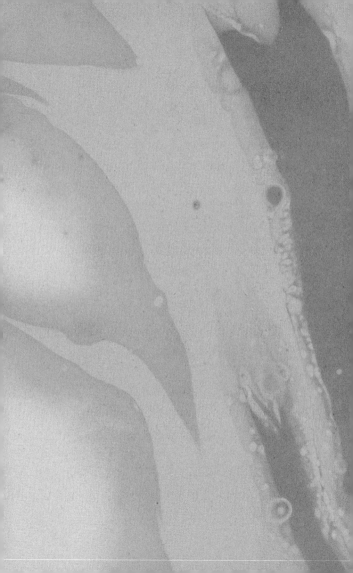

AN IMPORTANT NOTE

THIS GUIDE HELPS PARENTS learn more about the disturbing incidence of depression and anxiety disorders in the lives of young people. Like other parent guides in this series, it's a tool that provides knowledge, references, and faith-based encouragement on the subject to help parents connect with their kids. However, we do not pretend to be physicians, health-care providers, or even experts on these difficult matters. As such, this resource is *not* a substitute for medical advice or treatment. It can accompany and support steps recommended by a qualified health-care professional, but it is not meant to replace or preclude any diagnosis or treatment. Axis cannot be responsible for actions taken without professional medical guidance.

We cannot say it loud enough or often enough: **If you even suspect your child** has suicidal thoughts or plans, STOP READING THIS AND TAKE ACTION NOW. Contact your family physician and tell them your teen is at risk of suicide and must be seen immediately. If a doctor cannot see them right away for whatever reason, do not leave your child alone until they can be seen and evaluated by a health-care professional qualified to assess adolescent behavioral health. If necessary, take your child to the nearest emergency room or urgent care center, demand priority, and do not leave the physician's office until next steps are in place (such as referral to a specialist, assessments, evaluations, treatment plans, outpatient/inpatient programs, etc.).

If you even suspect
your child has suicidal
thoughts or plans, STOP
READING THIS AND TAKE
ACTION NOW.

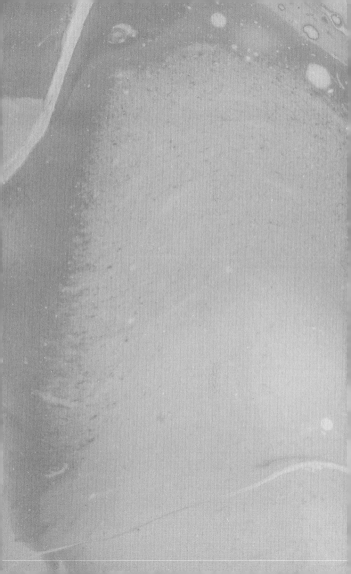

WHAT ARE DEPRESSION AND ANXIETY?

CLINICAL DEPRESSION AND ANXIETY disorders go far beyond "the blues," grief, tension with a cranky teacher, or irritation with a friend who didn't text back. When a person presents a severe, long-standing distortion in mood that doesn't match current circumstances, mental health-care professionals refer to it as a "depressive disorder" or an "anxiety disorder." These conditions, grouped into a category of illnesses called mood disorders or affective disorders, impact daily lifestyle, relationships, personality, and sometimes cognitive functioning.[3] They require professional medical care to resolve and, left untreated, can result in devastation for sufferers—and their loved ones.

Anxiety disorders are the most commonly diagnosed mental illness in the US, affecting more than 18 percent of the population every year.[4] Major depression carries the heaviest burden of disability; every year it affects more than 16 million adults and 2 million teens (ages twelve to seventeen) severely enough to impair their daily lives.[5] There are different forms of depression and anxiety, each of which affects a person differently and requires different approaches for treatment.[6]

Yet fewer than a third of those suffering from these very serious mental conditions ever receive treatment, despite the huge potential for successful treatment. At the same time, Lifeway Research reports that nearly half of evangelical, fundamentalist, or born-again Christians (48 percent) believe that people with depression, anxiety, and other serious mental illnesses can overcome their condition by praying more often, growing in spiritual maturity, or reading the Bible more.[7]

When a person presents a severe, long-standing distortion in mood that doesn't match current circumstances, mental health-care professionals refer to it as a "depressive disorder" or an "anxiety disorder."

ARE DEPRESSED AND ANXIOUS TEENS JUST EXPERIENCING NORMAL UPS AND DOWNS?

PSYCHIATRISTS BEGAN TO FOCUS on mood disorders in kids during the late 1980s, but they had trouble with diagnosis at first because kids don't always present the same symptoms as adults. Physicians and researchers now know that 14 percent—or 1 in 7—kids age ten through nineteen suffer from a mental health disorder.[8]

Psychology Today reports that "for almost 50 percent of patients, mental disorders start before they reach adulthood."[9] Neuropsychiatric conditions are the leading cause of disability in young people in every region on the planet. The World Mental Health Survey confirms this, showing that although many mental disorders begin in childhood or adolescence, "diagnosis and treatment may be delayed for years."[10] Stanford Medicine Children's Health says, "It's harder to spot mood disorders in children and teens. That's often because they are not always able to say how they feel."[11]

If left untreated, depression and anxiety disorders severely influence a person's development, their ability to achieve and succeed in education, and their hope of leading fulfilling, productive lives. Young people with mental disorders also must deal with stigma, isolation, and discrimination, as well as lack of access to health care and education facilities.[12]

Sadness, grief, fear, worry, distress, loneliness—it's true that these emotions should be expected during times of loss, failure, trauma, disappointment, and difficulty. Teens and health-care professionals refer to these as "triggers." Jesus Himself acknowledged the problems this world will bring us when He said, "In this world you *will have trouble*" (John 16:33, emphasis added). Jesus also understands our sufferings—He was described by Isaiah as "a man of suffering, and familiar with pain" (Isaiah 53:3).

Our "normal," everyday feelings can be overwhelming to say the least and must be properly explored. Teens may withdraw, cry, rage, refuse to eat, have trouble sleeping, etc. because of a difficult circumstance or painful experience; it does not necessarily mean they are mentally ill. A teen's mood swings can last a few minutes, hours, or days. As parents, we can and should teach our kids coping strategies and ways to obtain healthy support to prepare them for what Jesus spoke of as the world's trouble.

However, *mental illness can be distinguished from sadness, grief, and fear.*

When nothing seems
to help (even methods or
activities that used to help),
or when behavior changes
in a damaging way
for an extended season,
it's time to consider
a mood disorder.

Teens with depression can experience intense emotions and mood swings without any trigger at all.[13] The American Psychiatric Association indicates a mood disorder diagnosis is appropriate when symptoms are "out of proportion to the situation or age-inappropriate" and "hinder [a person's] ability to function normally."[14] In other words, when symptoms last weeks, when a person's identity is affected, when nothing seems to help (even methods or activities that used to help), or when behavior changes in a damaging way for an extended season, it's time to consider a mood disorder. By way of example, the APA explains how normal grief differs from major depression:

> In grief, painful feelings come in waves, often intermixed with positive memories of the deceased. In major depression,

mood and/or interest (pleasure)
are decreased for most of two
weeks. In grief, self-esteem
is usually maintained. In
major depression, feelings of
worthlessness and self-loathing
are common. . . . When grief and
depression co-occur, the grief is
more severe and lasts longer than
grief without depression.[15]

WHAT CAUSES DEPRESSION AND ANXIETY?

SOMETIMES THE PROBLEM can be traced to just one factor, but most often a combination of dynamics initiates mood disorders in teens. Physiologically speaking, a variety of factors, chemicals, and processes are involved.[16] Beyond that, mental health-care professionals say these illnesses can be triggered by or traced to:

- A high familial incidence of depression and/or anxiety

- Life events such as abuse, trauma, loss, or neglect

- Chronic high levels of stress

- Chronic physical illness such as cancer, diabetes, multiple sclerosis, or heart disease

- A high rate of metabolism of certain brain chemicals called neurotransmitters (such as

serotonin and dopamine) known to
regulate mood

- A dysfunction in the amygdala, the
  area of the brain where moods are
  controlled[17]

WHAT ARE THE SPIRITUAL RAMIFICATIONS?

IMMOBILIZED BY A COGNITIVE ASSASSIN, patients in the deepest throes of depression and anxiety have a hard time believing that God values and creates people with a purpose. Some believe their unbearable pain or numbness are character flaws. In some, their expectations and capabilities are irreconcilable, and symptoms get worse from the resulting frustration and embarrassment.

Because of all these factors, those with clinical depression or anxiety often understandably struggle in their relationship with God, which contributes to a downward spiral. When paired with bad advice from spiritual leaders (see next section), this can also cause them to doubt God's goodness or that He even exists. The sufferer may look for answers and solutions in other places that promise solace, comfort, and healing, but only lead to the opposite. However, when good spiritual advice is paired with good medical treatment, sufferers can find lasting physiological, spiritual, and emotional healing.

Immobilized by a cognitive assassin, patients in the deepest throes of depression and anxiety have a hard time believing that God values and creates people with a purpose.

HOW CAN MY CHURCH OR PASTOR HELP?

We have to break the stigma that causes people to say that people with mental illness are just of no value. . . . I think Christians have been slower than the population at large to recognize what mental illness is, let alone what they should do.

—ED STETZER, EXECUTIVE DIRECTOR OF THE WHEATON COLLEGE BILLY GRAHAM CENTER[18]

Unfortunately, current research confirms Christian churches aren't (yet) very good at supporting those with mental health issues.[19] And sadly, our experience at Axis is in line with the research. We've heard some pastors (though fewer and fewer every year) align psychiatry, psychology, and talk therapy with "witchcraft" or "sorcery," blaming emotional instability on the presence of unconfessed sin, spiritual immaturity, a lack of discipline, or a character flaw. Their advice to the depressed and anxious, therefore, tends to sound like this: "Repent, pray more, read more Scripture, and engage in spiritual disciplines." We've even heard directly from church leaders that "real Christians don't get depressed or anxious"—something about sin-guilt or a failure to grasp the redemptive power of God.

Pastor and author Frank Page explained the effects of our tendency to downplay and diminish mental illness in his book *Melissa: A Father's Lessons from a Daughter's Suicide*:

> We hear it sometimes stated in Christian circles that depression is a choice, that if you just snap out of it, talk yourself out of it, or pray yourself out of it, then you

In truth, usually church leaders cannot offer effective support to the mentally ill because they don't know how to help, not because they don't want to help.

won't have to deal with this. Or
we hear that depression is nothing
more than weakness, meaning
that you simply need to snap out
of it and get into a better way of
positive thinking. While some of
that may be true in some small
degree, I think we have often used
platitudes that fail to demonstrate
a true understanding about what
mental and emotional struggles
are really like. And so I tell people
to be very careful about your
platitudes, since they can be
hurtful, and they're inadequate in
almost every case.[20]

Yet the majority of those suffering from
a mental illness such as depression or
anxiety are hopeful and want church
leaders to talk more openly about it. In
truth, usually church leaders cannot

offer effective support to the mentally ill because they *don't know how* to help, not because they *don't want* to help. Lifeway Research found that two-thirds of Protestant senior pastors seldom speak to their congregations about mental illness, but they don't self-identify as "reluctant" to get involved with those suffering from acute mental illness. Pastors instead feel "overwhelmed" by it: "Pastors need more guidance and preparation for dealing with mental health crises. They often don't have a plan to help individuals or families affected by mental illness, and miss opportunities to be the church."[21] As Ed Stetzer put it, "Pastors are trained for spiritual struggle. They're not trained for mental illness."[22]

So take some time to talk to your pastor and find out what your church offers. If nothing is available, offer to work with the church and mental health experts to create a program that addresses all facets of the illness and properly equips church leaders to deal with mental illness. In doing so, you will be helping so many in your congregation get the spiritual and medical help they need.

HOW WILL I KNOW IF MY TEEN SUFFERS FROM DEPRESSION OR ANXIETY?

MOOD DISORDERS often have physically, emotionally, and spiritually troubling symptoms. Depression and anxiety can occur separately or at the same time, sometimes triggering and cycling through one another. Children and teens can also show different symptoms than adults (e.g., a depressed teen may seem more irritable than sad), and every individual who suffers from these illnesses will find a unique explanation for them.

That said, if the following common symptoms of depressive disorders persist for more than two weeks, it's probably time to seek professional help:

- Overwhelming feelings of sadness, restlessness, or apathy

- Decreased interest in activities (especially ones that used to be enjoyable)

- Trouble eating and sleeping (either too much or too little)

- Physical complaints like headaches, stomach pain, or muscle soreness

- Loss of energy or increased fatigue

- Increased hand-wringing or pacing, or noticeably slowed movements and speech

- Excessive feelings of worthlessness, guilt, hopelessness, inadequacy, or shame

- Difficulty concentrating, focusing, or making decisions

- Thoughts or statements of wanting to die[23]

Anxiety disorders involve "persistent, excessive fear or worry in situations that are not necessarily threatening." Teens often avoid situations that trigger or worsen their symptoms, which can include:

- Apprehension or dread that makes them change their plans or avoid places or people

- Tension or jumpiness

- Restlessness or irritability

- Increased feelings of vigilance (anticipation of the worst, watching for danger signs)

- Pounding or racing heartbeat

- Shortness of breath

- Headaches

- Trouble sleeping despite feeling fatigued

- Upset stomach or even diarrhea

- Sweating or tremors[24]

Anxiety can also manifest as panic disorder (characterized by sudden feelings of terror sometimes mistaken for a heart attack), phobias (when an event, object, or place triggers a powerful, irrational fear response), and social anxiety disorder—not shyness, but an intense, irrational fear of social situations.

Other signs of mood disorders in teens may include academic difficulties, hostility or rage, rebellion, thoughts or threats of running away, hypersensitivity to failure or rejection, and trouble relating to others.[25]

When prolonged and left untreated, these disorders can effectively numb the brain from all feeling as a protective measure. This makes it difficult to accomplish the smallest of tasks, such as getting out of bed or maintaining personal hygiene. The most severe cases hinder concentration so that coherent thoughts are impossible.

Depression and anxiety can occur separately or at the same time, sometimes triggering and cycling through one another. . . . Anxiety disorders involve "persistent, excessive fear or worry in situations that are not necessarily threatening."

—NATIONAL ALLIANCE ON MENTAL ILLNESS

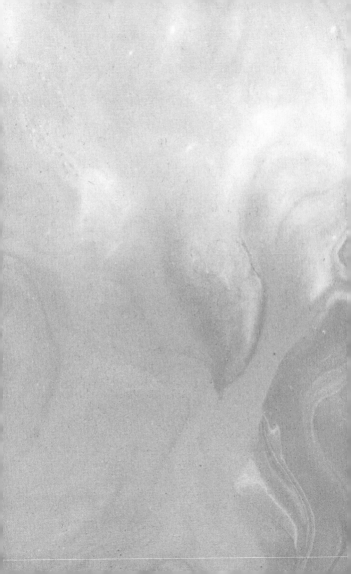

WHAT TYPES OF TREATMENTS ARE THERE?

DEPRESSION AND ANXIETY CAN BE effectively treated, and the earlier treatment begins, the better the prognosis: quality of life can improve drastically in a fairly short time. Yet many of those diagnosed with major depression (including adults) never receive any treatment for it, and even fewer receive *good* treatment. So rather than prolonging our teens' misery, let's help them by providing treatment that addresses all facets of the problem.

The value of prayer, study, meditation, etc. as *one part* of treatment cannot be overestimated, and unacknowledged sin, a weak relationship with God, brokenness, abuse, or trauma will all have negative consequences in one's life. However, mental illnesses stem from neurochemical depletions and imbalances. These don't respond to our will to fix them, no matter how hard we try.[26] Besides, spiritual discipline requires concentration that often isn't possible in the throes of a severe mood disorder. Telling a critically depressed person to "read more Scripture" or "pray harder" is like asking them to flip on a lamp with a burned-out bulb; it's not going to light up, no matter how many times they try.

With that in mind, both faith leaders and parents shouldn't try to diagnose, treat, or cure *any* illness, let alone mental illness. In addition, no single method of healing is a one-size-fits-all treatment, so what worked for one teen may not work for the next. This is important for us all to remember because an inappropriate spiritual rebuke can affect the life, and even the eternity, of someone fighting a debilitating mental illness.

Mood disorders can share symptoms with other illnesses, so only a health-care professional with experience in treating child and adolescent mental illnesses can detect and treat these disorders properly. A complete psychiatric evaluation (including information about your child's medical history, family history, age, social experience, and other factors) can narrow the possibilities and result in an accurate diagnosis and a more effective treatment plan, which may include the following options:

- Talk therapy to uncover and address unhealthy beliefs and thought patterns

- Medications (especially when combined with talk therapy)

- Medical and psychiatric testing (including emotional inventories, physical exams, genetic testing, and others)

- Holistic approaches (such as lifestyle changes, training in self-care, or natural supplements)

- Inpatient, residential, or outpatient treatment programs, particularly if suicidal ideation or dangerous behavior persists[27]

- Meditation or mindfulness-based cognitive therapy, which studies are showing can be as effective in treating depression as medications[28]

- In severe or prolonged cases, transcranial magnetic stimulation or electroconvulsive therapy (don't worry—these treatments are nothing like *One Flew Over the Cuckoo's Nest*. Ask your doctor for an explanation.)

Telling a critically depressed person to "read more Scripture" or "pray harder" is like asking them to flip on a lamp with a burned-out bulb; it's not going to light up, no matter how many times they try.

Family and friends play a vital supporting role in your child's treatment, management, and recovery from these illnesses. Family members may even accompany the teen to talk therapy sessions, attend group therapy sessions, or receive their own private therapy sessions, if deemed helpful.

The most important thing you can do: effectively weigh the pros and cons of all treatment methods in partnership with a health-care provider experienced in adolescent mental health and treatment. Talk to the doctor about how medication can specifically help your teen, and don't forget to tell the physician about other prescribed or over-the-counter medications your teen takes.

Christ Himself—although well known for miraculous healings with just a word or a touch—employed a variety of techniques similar to treatment regimens, medicines, talk therapy, and other common methods of mental health care. Of course, He could have healed any way He pleased; His example shows how grace and individualized care leads to the wholeness He wants for us all (see John 10:10).

HOW CAN I SUPPORT MY TEEN'S TREATMENT?

CARE FOR THEIR PHYSICAL NEEDS.

In 1 Kings 19, after a significant spiritual victory, Elijah collapsed under a tree and told God he was ready to die. God answered Elijah by first providing for his immediate, most basic needs: food, water, and rest. Renowned missionary Mother Teresa also focused first on the felt needs of people, knowing each part of human wholeness—physical, mental, emotional, and spiritual—is indelibly linked to the other parts.

Even if a mental illness has damaged your teen's physical health (poor eating habits, lack of sleep, poor hygiene, no motivation to exercise, etc.), encourage and even facilitate activity in their life. Agree with them that it's difficult, but remind them how even a little activity can deflect symptoms and ward off an episode. You might even assign a loved one to account for the ill person physically from day to day. Just getting them out of the house for a while can do the trick.

HELP THEM PRAY—AND PRAY FOR THEM.

People with mood disorders often cannot manage praying for themselves. Although the Spirit will intercede for them with "wordless groans" (Romans 8:26), the intercession of the body of Christ can put words to often-inexplicable suffering and validate your teen and their illness. Encourage others who can protect the situation's confidentiality to intercede in prayer, both in their own prayers and with your teen. Intercessory prayer will offer support when the healing process stalls or hits a snag.

ENCOURAGE OR ASSIST THEM IN ACCURATELY ASSESSING THE ISSUE.

Make an appointment with a qualified physician—not just any caregiver, but a specialist in adolescent behavioral illness.

As mentioned earlier, mood disorders are actually very common and very treatable. Cheer your teen on as they pursue healing through treatment.

ASSURE THEM OF GOD'S TRUTH.

People with mood disorders often forget what joy feels like. Their unmet expectations of life and what may seem like personal failure can arrest them with guilt and ruminating negative thoughts. Gently remind them of God's love, grace, power, and promises, correcting any distorted beliefs and thwarting their mind's destructive messaging. The gospel is a story of something already done, not something we must do, and God's truth is independent of our perception; that is, the truth is true *not* because of who hears it but because of who declares it! A clear understanding of this removes our responsibility of being "good enough" or "holy enough" and allows us to rest in the One who did it all (see Matthew 11:28-30).

BE VULNERABLE.

Philosopher Jean Vanier said it best in his book *Community and Growth*: "I am struck by how sharing our weakness and difficulties is more nourishing to others than sharing our qualities and successes."[29] If you've ever struggled with depression, anxiety, suicidal thoughts, or anything that made you doubt God's goodness, don't hide that from your teen. Knowing they're not alone and that someone else has struggled or is struggling in the same way can make all the difference. Share what you've learned and how it's strengthened your faith and trust in God, too, not just the struggles you've had.

GIVE THEM SPECIFIC STEPS TO COMBAT A SERIOUS EPISODE.

Quality of life for the mentally ill can be cyclical, with good days and bad days. Bad days occur unexpectedly and ruthlessly, with or without "triggers" or explanations. On a good day, provide a written list of spiritual helps for when bad days rear their nasty heads. You might list heartening Bible passages, words for prayer, God's promises, names and phone numbers of supportive people to call, etc. *Emphasize perseverance rather than achievement.* A physical, written list—one they can see and touch—will help focus their racing mind and tangibly prove that someone cares and support exists.

MINISTER TO CAREGIVERS.

Families and loved ones can suffer greatly, particularly if they've had no (or not much) experience with psychiatric care or mental illness themselves. They may feel out of control, angry, bitter, worried, burdened, impatient, helpless, or any number of complicated emotions. If your teen knows someone in trouble or if you know of a parent with a struggling teen themselves, provide support to them separately, ministering to their unique spiritual needs as you uncover them.

Don't forget, dear parent, that *you are a caregiver*. You must not allow your compassion or actions on the behalf of your suffering child to drain you of your own personal wholeness. Acknowledge your own needs and boundaries, and like Elijah, allow your relationship with God and others to refill and renew you. Not only will you be caring for yourself in stewardship of the vessel God gave you; this will also set a good example to those who are watching (and healing).

If you've ever struggled with depression, anxiety, suicidal thoughts, or anything that made you doubt God's goodness, don't hide that from your teen ... "sharing our weakness and difficulties is more nourishing to others than sharing our qualities and successes."

—JEAN VANIER

BE PATIENT.

Mental illnesses, like mood disorders, are treatable, but effective treatment can be a long, variable, complicated journey. Despite the high success rate of psychological treatment, the illness itself can affect the drive to seek help. (It can feel safer to remain ill than to do the hard, unfamiliar work of getting better.) Your teen may also get impatient and frustrated if they learn that initial treatment choices need adjustment. While remembering to prioritize your self-care, pledge not to abandon your teen on their road to wholeness. Repeat helpful biblical truths as many times as necessary. (Depression and anxiety can make things hard to remember.) Perseverance will uncover all kinds of opportunities for spiritual growth in them and in you, and God will be glorified by them.

REFER CRISES OR THE CRITICALLY ILL TO EMERGENCY CARE.

Some cases may be so severe or may have gone untreated for so long that your assistance (and these suggestions) will not suffice. You might discover evidence that your teen could be a danger to themselves or others. As terrifying as this idea is, parents must take all suggestions of self-harm, suicide, homicide, or unlawful acts very seriously. In these cases and for your child's sake, make safety a priority. Call 911 and/or seek acute intervention immediately. A local inpatient behavioral treatment center, urgent care center, or hospital emergency room is best equipped to provide this help.

If you want to make this kind of help more widely available, ask your pastor to keep information on local emergency care options handy and updated. Make sure your pastor knows which hospitals specialize in emotional crisis intervention, and suggest that lay volunteer leaders be trained to contact the pastor immediately when they observe dangerous behavior or evidence of an emotional crisis in the church body.

A FINAL
ENCOURAGEMENT

WHEN MOOD DISORDERS like depression, anxiety, and other serious mental illnesses become manageable in a Christian who has long suffered, it is experienced as a holy deliverance from a very personal sort of pain. It activates a spiritual light that burns bright and won't be extinguished by the failings of this fallen world. Their agony melts into a symphony of life inside someone who once was desperate just to plink out a few notes of it. Author and pastor John Ortberg said it like this in his book *The Life You've Always Wanted*: "Often it is the people closest to suffering who have the most powerful joy."[30]

With your help and a well-executed treatment program, your struggling teen can uncover incredible joy buried under these very real, very dangerous illnesses and reach the abundant life promised by Christ. It's desperately needed, easier than you think, and so worth it.

> We need to be angels for each other, to give each other strength and consolation. Because only when we fully realize that the cup of life is not only a cup of sorrow but also a cup of joy will we be able to drink it.

—HENRI NOUWEN[31]

RECAP

- Anxiety and depression are mood disorders that can affect a person starting as early as age eleven.

- Mental illnesses are different from normal emotions because they happen without a trigger, are out of proportion with the situation, are age-inappropriate, or hinder a person's ability to function normally.

- There are a variety of factors that can cause depression and anxiety, including genetics, trauma, chemical imbalances, and chronic illness.

- Sufferers can struggle in their relationships with God, and the church can add to this problem by saying that real Christians don't get depressed or anxious.

- It's important to seek professional help if the symptoms of depression or anxiety persist for longer than two weeks.

- It's important to talk with both health-care professionals and trusted spiritual leaders to develop a well-rounded treatment plan.

- Be actively involved in your child's treatment by praying for and with them, reminding them of God's truth, caring for their physical needs, being patient and vulnerable, and seeking emergency care when appropriate.

DISCUSSION QUESTIONS

1. Have you or has anyone you know ever struggled with depression? Anxiety? What did you or they do to deal with it?

2. How do your friends talk about mental health issues? Do you have someone besides me that you can talk to if you're struggling?

3. How do you feel when talking about mental health?

4. Do you wish our church/pastors talked about mental health more or differently? If so, how and why?

5. What can I do differently to show you that I care about your mental health and do not think less of you if you struggle?

6. What does the Bible say about dealing with sorrows and worries?

How can that help us when we're in the midst of depression or anxiety?

7. Has anyone ever given you unhelpful advice for dealing with mental health? Why did you find it unhelpful? What would be better?

8. How can you and I be more aware of other people's mental and emotional struggles? How can we help them mentally, physically, and spiritually?

ADDITIONAL RESOURCES

1. National Institute of Mental Health (NIMH): Depression and Anxiety Disorders, https://www.nimh.nih.gov /health/topics/depression and https:// www.nimh.nih.gov/health/topics /anxiety-disorders

2. National Alliance on Mental Illness (NAMI): Depression and Anxiety Disorders, https://www.nami.org /About-Mental-Illness/Mental-Health -Conditions/Depression and https:// www.nami.org/About-Mental-Illness /Mental-Health-Conditions/Anxiety -Disorders

3. American Psychiatric Association: Depression and Anxiety Disorders, https://www.psychiatry.org/patients -families/depression/what-is-depression and https://www.psychiatry.org/patients -families/anxiety-disorders/what-are -anxiety-disorders

4. Mental Health Ministries, mentalhealthministries.net

5. Anxiety & Depression Association of America (ADAA), https://adaa.org/

6. The Mighty: Mental Health, https://
   themighty.com/topic/mental-health/

7. Mental Health America's Depression
   Screening Tool, https://screening.
   mhanational.org/screening-tools
   /depression/

8. World Health Organization on depression,
   https://www.who.int/en/news-room/fact
   -sheets/detail/depression

9. Saddleback Church's "Mental Health
   Resource Guide for Individuals and
   Families," http://www.mentalhealth
   ministries.net/resources/resource
   _guides/Hope_Resource_Guide.pdf

10. "Mental Illness & Medication vs. Spiritual
    Struggles & Biblical Counseling," https://
    pastors.com/meds-vs-spiritual/

11. "7 Things to NEVER Say to a Depressed
    Christian," https://churchleaders.com
    /outreach-missions/outreach-missions
    -articles/249798-7-things-never-say
    -depressed-christian.html

12. "Depression: Reject the Guilt, Embrace
    the Cure," https://www.focusonthefamily

.com/marriage/depression-reject-the
-guilt-embrace-the-cure/

13. "Too Depressed to Believe What
    We Know: Eleven Resources for the
    Darkness," https://www.desiringgod.org
    /articles/too-depressed-to-believe-what
    -we-know

14. "5 Things Christians Should Know
    about Depression and Anxiety," https://
    relevantmagazine.com/life5/5-things
    -christians-should-know-about
    -depression-and-anxiety/

15. "Top 10 Resources for Mental Health
    Ministry," https://www.christianitytoday
    .com/pastors/2016/april-web-exclusives
    /top-10-resources-for-mental-health
    -ministry.html

16. National Suicide Prevention Lifeline,
    https://988lifeline.org/ or call 988

17. Suicide Awareness Voices of Education
    (SAVE), https://save.org/ or call 988

NOTES

1. Sarah Eekhoff Zylstra, "1 in 4 Pastors Have Struggled with Mental Illness, Finds LifeWay and Focus on the Family," *Christianity Today*, September 22, 2014, https://www.christianity today.com/news/2014/september/1-in-4 -pastors-have-mental-illness-lifeway-focus -on-family.html.

2. "A Point of View: Churchill, Chance and the 'Black Dog,'" BBC News, September 23, 2011, https://www.bbc.com/news/magazine -15033046.

3. "Mood Disorders," Mental Health America, accessed September 21, 2022, https://www. mhanational.org/conditions/mood-disorders; "Mood Disorders in Teens," Stanford Medicine Children's Health, accessed September 21, 2022, https://www.stanfordchildrens.org/en /topic/default?id=overview-of-mood-disorders -in-children-and-adolescents-90-P01634.

4. "Anxiety Disorders – Facts & Statistics," Anxiety & Depression Association of America, accessed September 21, 2022, https://adaa .org/understanding-anxiety/facts-statistics.

5. Jonaki Bose et al., "Key Substance Use and Mental Health Indicators in the United States: Results from the 2015 National Survey on Drug Use and Health," Substance Abuse and Mental Health Services Administration, September 2016, https://www.samhsa.gov/data/sites/default/files/NSDUH-FFR1-2015/NSDUH-FFR1-2015/NSDUH-FFR1-2015.htm.

6. "Depression," National Institute of Mental Health, September 2022, https://www.nimh.nih.gov/health/topics/depression; "What Are the Five Major Types of Anxiety Disorders?" HHS.gov, February 12, 2014, https://www.hhs.gov/answers/mental-health-and-substance-abuse/what-are-the-five-major-types-of-anxiety-disorders/index.html.

7. Bob Smietana, "Mental Illness Remains Taboo Topic for Many Pastors," Lifeway Research, September 22, 2014, https://research.lifeway.com/2014/09/22/mental-illness-remains-taboo-topic-for-many-pastors/.

8. "Adolescent Mental Health," World Health Organization, November 17, 2021, https://www.who.int/news-room/fact-sheets/detail/adolescent-mental-health.

9. Sebastian Ocklenburg, "At What Age Does Mental Illness Begin?" *Psychology Today*, June 18, 2021, https://www.psychologytoday.com/us/blog/the-asymmetric-brain/202106/what-age-does-mental-illness-begin.

10. "Mental Health Issues," World Health Organization, accessed September 21, 2022, https://apps.who.int/adolescent/second-decade/section4/page1/Mental-health-issues.html.

11. "Mood Disorders in Teens."

12. Christina Halli, "Mood Disorders in Teens Is Not Normal Moodiness," March 1, 2015, https://www.healthyplace.com/blogs/parentingchildwithmentalillness/2015/03/mood-disorders-in-teens.

13. Halli, "Mood Disorders in Teens."

14. "What Are Anxiety Disorders?" American Psychiatric Association, accessed October 2, 2022, https://psychiatry.org/patients-families/anxiety-disorders/what-are-anxiety-disorders.

15. "What Is Depression?" American Psychiatric Association, accessed October 2, 2022, https://psychiatry.org/patients-families/depression/what-is-depression.

16. "What Causes Depression?" Harvard Health Publishing, January 10, 2022, https://www.health.harvard.edu/mind-and-mood/what-causes-depression.

17. Debra Fulghum Bruce, "Causes of Depression," WebMD, March 8, 2021, https://www.webmd.com/depression/guide/causes-depression and "What Causes Depression?" Harvard Health Publishing, January 10, 2022, https://www.health.harvard.edu/mind-and-mood/what-causes-depression.

18. Zylstra, "1 in 4 Pastors Have Struggled with Mental Illness."

19. Smietana, "Mental Illness Remains Taboo Topic."

20. Frank Page with Lawrence Kimbrough, *Melissa: A Father's Lessons from a Daughter's Suicide* (Nashville: B&H Books, 2013).

21. Smietana, "Mental Illness Remains Taboo Topic."

22. Zylstra, "1 in 4 Pastors Have Struggled with Mental Illness."

23. "What Is Depression?"

24. "Anxiety Disorders," National Alliance on Mental Illness, accessed September 21, 2022, https://www.nami.org/About-Mental-Illness /Mental-Health-Conditions/Anxiety-Disorders.

25. "Mood Disorders in Teens."

26. "What Causes Depression?"

27. "Mood Disorder Treatment Program Options," PsychGuides.com, accessed September 21, 2022, https://www.psychguides.com/mood -disorders/treatment/.

28. Stacy Lu, "Mindfulness Holds Promise for Treating Depression," American Psychological Association, March 2015, https://www.apa .org/monitor/2015/03/cover-mindfulness; Sarah Knapton, "Mindfulness Can Control Depression as Well as Drugs, Study Shows," *Telegraph*, April 27, 2016, https://www .telegraph.co.uk/science/2016/04/27/ mindfulness-can-control-depression-as-well -as-drugs-study-shows/.

29. Jean Vanier, *Community and Growth* (Mahwah, NJ: Paulist Press, 1989), 185.

30. John Ortberg, *The Life You've Always Wanted: Spiritual Disciplines for Ordinary People* (Grand Rapids, MI: Zondervan, 2002), 248.

31. Henri J. M. Nouwen, *Can You Drink the Cup?* (Notre Dame, IN: Ave Maria Press, 2006), 56.

PARENT GUIDES TO SOCIAL MEDIA
BY AXIS

It's common to feel lost in your teen's world. Let these be your go-to guides on social media, how it affects your teen, and how to begin an ongoing conversation about faith that matters.

BUNDLE THESE 5 BOOKS AND SAVE